THE LADIES HAVE LE*f*T THE BUILDING

ALFRESCO FARE FOR EATING IN
THE BEST PLACE OF ALL—OUT

Eating out is *in*.

Haven't you heard?

Everything tastes better outside.

Which is why we've
conjured up a whole book of
alfresco (a.k.a. the great outdoors)
eats and ideas, complete with
six tasty menus that'll take you
from the beach to the backyard and
from sunny skies to starry nights.

So grab that picnic basket.
Kick off those shoes.

And prepare to eat somewhere special.

OUT.

TABLE *of* CONTENTS

note: for food safety info, visit www.foodsafety.gov.

CHOPST*i*CKS
in the PARK

Far East flavors and too-cute takeout containers make this a picnic of very good fortune.

MANGO-VEGGIE SUMMER ROLLS

Summer does have a taste in these crunchy, fresh rolls and their sweet dipping sauce.

4 ounces bean thread or glass noodles

1 tablespoon toasted sesame oil

1 mango, peeled and julienned

1 large carrot, peeled and julienned

1 medium zucchini, peeled and julienned

1 bunch green onions, white and light green parts only, julienned

½ cup bean sprouts, washed and dried

1 cup tightly packed mixed herbs such as mint, cilantro and Thai basil

8 Boston lettuce leaves, ribs removed

¼ cup finely chopped, roasted, unsalted peanuts

16 8-inch rice paper wraps

DIPPING SAUCE

6 tablespoons fish sauce

2 tablespoons sugar

5 tablespoons lime juice

1½ tablespoons garlic chili paste

Cut the noodles into 3-inch pieces and soak in cold water for 30 minutes. Drain and plunge into hot water for 1 minute. Drain again and rinse with cold water. Place in a small bowl and toss with the sesame oil.

Set all ingredients except for rice paper wraps out separately in assembly-line fashion. In a small bowl, mix together the dipping sauce ingredients. Have a large shallow bowl of lukewarm water close by. Place a clean dish towel in front of you.

Dip one rice paper wrap in the water for about 30 seconds, remove and place on the dish towel. Line bottom third of wrap with a small amount of lettuce, then noodles, then mango, followed by a small amount of each of the vegetables and the herbs. Top with a light sprinkle of peanuts and a small drizzle of the dipping sauce. Tightly fold in the sides then roll from the bottom up. Continue with remaining wraps and ingredients. Cut each roll in half and serve with the remaining sauce.

Cook's Tip: Rolls can be prepared up to 4 hours in advance. Wrap in plastic and store covered in a single layer inside an airtight container.

CRUNCHY SESAME WONTON CRISPS

Wonton wrappers debut as crispy, baked crackers kissed with sesame seeds and salt.

1 4-inch piece of fresh ginger

¼ teaspoon cayenne pepper

1 egg yolk

2 tablespoons milk

1 tablespoon vegetable oil

48 square wonton wrappers

1 tablespoon black sesame seeds

1 tablespoon hulled sesame seeds

1 tablespoon sea salt flakes

PEANUT DIPPING SAUCE

½ cup smooth peanut butter

2 tablespoons fish sauce

3 tablespoons fresh lime juice

½ teaspoon sugar

1 teaspoon garlic chili paste

5 tablespoons water

Preheat oven to 350°F. Set racks to center and top third of oven. Line 2 baking sheets with parchment paper.

Finely grate the ginger, then strain through a fine sieve. Keep the juice and discard the pulp (you should have 3 tablespoons of ginger juice). In a small bowl, whisk together the ginger juice, cayenne pepper, egg yolk and milk. Set egg glaze aside.

Brush one side of each wonton wrapper with oil, and place, oil-side down, on prepared baking sheets. Brush the tops of each wonton with the egg glaze and sprinkle with a combination of both sesame seeds. Sprinkle lightly with the salt. Bake for 7-8 minutes or until wontons are crisp and golden. Transfer to a wire rack. Cool completely.

For the peanut sauce, combine all ingredients in a small bowl, mixing until thoroughly combined. Serve with the wonton crisps.

ASIAN PEPPERED SALMON

A medley of Asian-inspired spices gives this salmon—and your picnic—some added kick.

¾ cup dried, unsweetened, shredded coconut
¼ cup blanched almonds
2 teaspoons coriander seeds
1 teaspoon Szechuan peppercorns
1 teaspoon sea salt flakes
1 2-pound salmon fillet, skin removed
2 teaspoons vegetable oil
Lime wedges as garnish

Preheat oven to 350°F. On parchment-lined baking sheets, lightly toast the coconut, almonds and spices separately until golden. The times will vary from 5 to 15 minutes (almonds will take the longest). Allow the ingredients to cool, add the salt, then grind in a spice grinder. Spread in a shallow bowl.

Pat the fish dry and cut into 8 1½-inch-wide pieces. Brush with oil, then evenly coat with the coconut mixture. Let stand at room temperature for 30 minutes.

Heat a large grill pan until hot, then rub with oil. Add the salmon and cook for 4 minutes on each side; if blackening too much, transfer to a baking sheet and finish cooking in the oven (preheated to 400°F) for 5 minutes, or until desired doneness is reached. Remove from heat and let cool completely. Serve with lime wedges.

Cook's Tip: To transport to picnic, wrap each cooked piece of salmon in wax paper, then heavy-duty aluminum foil. Carry in an ice chest. Allow the fish to stand at room temperature for 10 minutes before serving.

ANATOMY OF A PICNIC BASKET

Plates?
"Check."

Cups, napkins, silverware?
"Check, check and double check."

Mints, matches and paper fans?
Oh.

Avoid the most common picnic pitfall of
them all—forgotten necessities.
Since there's nothing worse than a cooler
full of bottles and no bottle opener,
we've laid out all the don't-forgets and
don't-be-caught-withouts.

So now your next picnic can be a big "do."

. . . .

☐ PICNIC BASKET

☐ A BLANKET OR
A RUG

☐ PLAYING CARDS
AND/OR DICE

☐ PLASTIC CUPS

☐ BOTTLE OPENER

☐ HOT OR COLD (OR
BOTH!) THERMOS

☐ NAPKINS

☐ MATCHES

☐ PLASTIC
SILVERWARE

☐ TRASH BAGS

☐ MINTS

☐ PAPER FAN

☐ A SUNHAT

☐ BATTERY-
OPERATED RADIO

☐ SHARP KNIFE

☐ BEACH TOWEL

☐ A FLASHLIGHT

☐ SALT + PEPPER

SOOO GOOD SOBA NOODLE SALAD

Cool noodles, crunchy cucumber, tangy lime and a pinch of chili—it really is **sooo** *good.*

12 ounces soba noodles
2 tablespoons safflower oil
1 tablespoon toasted sesame oil
Finely grated zest of 2 limes
Juice of 3 limes
1 tablespoon sugar
2 tablespoons fish sauce
1 finely chopped green chili
2 English cucumbers,* peeled, seeded and halved lengthwise
4 tablespoons Thai basil leaves or fresh mint leaves, shredded

Bring a large pot of salted water to a boil. Add the noodles and gently push all the noodles into the water in long strands. Return to a boil, reduce heat and simmer for 4 minutes, stirring occasionally to prevent noodles from sticking together.

Meanwhile, in a small bowl mix together the oils, lime zest and juice, sugar and fish sauce. Whisk until sugar is dissolved. Add the chili. Drain the noodles, rinse with cold water and place on a large baking sheet. Pour the dressing over the noodles, tossing with tongs to coat. Let cool completely, tossing occasionally.

Using a mandoline, slice the cucumber into long, thin strands. Add to the noodles. Mix in the basil or mint leaves. Let stand for at least 20 minutes before serving.

*English cucumbers are also often called "seedless" or "hothouse."

Cook's Tip: Salad can be prepared and refrigerated up to 1 day in advance.

THE SKINNY ON *soba*

Soba noodles (soba is the Japanese word for "buckwheat") have become one of Japan's most popular fast-food fares. Commuters often zip in to snag a quick serving at places like train stations where, standing up, they loudly slurp down their noodles. Slurping, you say? That's correct. In most Asian cultures, all that noisemaking isn't considered impolite at all. In fact, it's believed that by sucking in air you actually enhance the dish's flavors. One other fun soba noodle fact: every New Year's, Japanese slurp down a bowl of these long, skinny noodles to ensure a long life.

LUCKY CHOCOLATE-APRICOT TARTS

One bite of these creamy truffle gems with their hidden apricot centers,
and you'll see why we call them lucky.

PASTRY

1⅔ cups all-purpose flour
2 tablespoons good-quality cocoa powder
Pinch of salt
1 tablespoon confectioners' sugar
1 stick unsalted butter, chilled and diced
2 egg yolks
4 tablespoons ice-cold water

FILLING

⅓ cup plus 2 tablespoons all-purpose flour
2 heaping tablespoons good-quality cocoa powder
Pinch of salt
½ cup firmly packed dark brown sugar
1 stick unsalted butter
4 ounces bittersweet chocolate, broken into pieces
1 vanilla bean, seeds scraped out, pod discarded
½ cup water
1 large egg
3 tablespoons apricot preserves
Cocoa powder for dusting
Fresh apricots as garnish

For the pastry, sift the flour, cocoa powder, salt and sugar into the bowl of a food processor. Add the butter and pulse until the mixture resembles breadcrumbs. In a separate bowl, mix together the egg yolks and water. Gradually add to flour mixture, pulsing until large clumps form. Turn out onto a clean surface and gently knead until smooth. Cover with plastic wrap and refrigerate for 30 minutes.

Preheat oven to 400°F. Set oven rack to top third of oven. Place a baking sheet in the oven to preheat. On a lightly floured surface, roll out the chilled dough to about ⅛ inch thick. Using a 4-inch-diameter round pastry cutter, cut out 12 discs of dough. Press each disc into 12 individual brioche or muffin tins (about 3 inches in diameter). Prick the base of each pastry with a fork. Chill for 20 minutes.

Remove pastry-lined tins from refrigerator. Line each pastry with parchment paper and fill with pie weights. Place tins on preheated baking sheet and bake for 10 minutes. Remove paper and weights and continue baking for an additional 5 minutes until pastry is completely set and crisp. Remove from oven. Reduce temp to 350°F.

Meanwhile, for the filling, sift the flour, cocoa powder and salt into a small bowl and make a well in the center. In a small saucepan over medium-low heat, combine the sugar, butter, chocolate, vanilla seeds and ½ cup water. Stir continuously until sugar dissolves and the butter and chocolate melt, about 5 minutes. Pour into the center of the dry ingredients and beat together until smooth. Add egg, mixing until combined.

Divide the apricot preserves between the pastry cups, then top with the chocolate mixture, filling ⅔ full. Return to oven and bake until tops are just set, about 3 minutes. Remove from oven. The tarts will fully set once they're completely cool. Dust with cocoa powder and serve at room temperature with fresh apricots.

A SHORE THING

Tuck your toes in the sand and get ready to feast by the sea with this picnic of beachside bites.

GRILLED SEASHELLS *by* THE SHORE

GRILLED SEASHELLS *by* THE SHORE

Mussels, clams and oysters meet the grill and three very succulent sauces.

1 pound large mussels
1 pound clams
24 oysters

CHIMICHURRI SAUCE
½ cup flat-leaf parsley, finely chopped
½ cup cilantro, finely chopped
2 tablespoons fresh oregano, finely chopped
½ teaspoon ground cumin
2 garlic cloves, peeled and crushed with 1 tsp sea salt flakes
⅓ cup extra-virgin olive oil
2 tablespoons sherry or red wine vinegar

GARLIC BUTTER
1 stick unsalted butter
3 garlic cloves, peeled and crushed with 2 tsp sea salt flakes
½ teaspoon cayenne pepper

RED ONION VINAIGRETTE
1 small red onion, finely chopped
¼ cup white wine vinegar
1 teaspoon sugar
1 teaspoon pink peppercorns, crushed
½ cup extra-virgin olive oil
Sea salt and freshly ground black pepper

Lime wedges, sea salt flakes and crushed black pepper for garnish

Wash all the shellfish, removing any grit. Debeard the mussels. If any shellfish are open, gently tap their shells. Discard any that do not close.

Make the dressings: For the Chimichurri Sauce, mix all ingredients together in a small bowl. Let stand for 30 minutes. For the Garlic Butter, melt the butter in a small pan over the grill. Add the garlic and cayenne and cook for 2 minutes until just sizzling. Serve warm. For the Red Onion Vinaigrette, mix the onion and vinegar together in a small bowl. Let stand for 10 minutes. Stir in the sugar and peppercorns, then whisk in the oil. Season to taste with salt and pepper.

Preheat the grill, placing rack 4-6 inches above the coals. If the mussels are small, you may need to place a grill pan or baking sheet on the rack and place the mussels inside it so they do not fall through the grill rack. Place the clams and oysters on the grill, making sure they don't touch and that they rest on their deeply curved sides to prevent their juices from leaking out as they open.

Grill until shellfish open and are fully cooked, about 3 minutes for the mussels and clams (6 minutes if using a baking sheet) and about 4 minutes for the oysters. The mussels and clams will open fully while the oysters will open only slightly. As shellfish open, take them off the grill and remove the inside meat. Serve immediately with sauces, lime wedges, salt and pepper.

Cook's Tip: Shellfish can be washed and prepped in advance. Pack on ice in a cooler to transport. The Chimichurri Sauce and Garlic Butter can be prepared up to 1 day in advance. The Red Onion Vinaigrette can be prepared up to 4 hours in advance. For the Chimichurri Sauce, mix together all ingredients except for the herbs; add 30 minutes before ready to serve. For the Garlic Butter, fold all the ingredients into softened butter, roll in parchment paper and chill. To use, simply melt in a pan just before serving.

shellfish SAFETY

Ensure a more fabulous (not to mention safe!) seaside feast by following these simple guidelines for buying, storing and cooking fresh shellfish.

When buying hard-shell mussels, oysters and clams, look for shells that are tightly shut. Gently tap any partially open shells—if they're still alive and edible, they should immediately close shut. Discard or do not buy any that remain open.

Avoid shellfish that smell fishy. Instead, look for a clean, fresh, salt-water aroma.

Try to enjoy your fresh shellfish as soon as possible after purchase. If you must store them, always keep them between 35°F and 40°F and no longer than 48-72 hours.

Refrigerate mussels, oysters and clams in bowls covered with a damp cloth. Placing them in airtight containers or fresh water will kill them.

When cooking, watch for shells to pop open slightly. As they do, remove each from the grill and continue cooking until all are opened. Discard any that remain closed.

ORANGE-SCENTED FENNEL + OLIVE SNAPPER

You'll feel like you've brought a present to the feast with this beautifully layered, not to mention insanely delicious, snapper.

1 fennel bulb, trimmed with fronds reserved
¾ cup kalamata olives, pitted and halved
1 small red onion, thinly sliced
2 oranges, peeled and cut into ¼-inch-thick slices
1 cup tightly packed flat-leaf parsley, chopped
2 tablespoons extra-virgin olive oil
Sea salt flakes and freshly ground black pepper
4 large red snapper fillets, about 1½ pounds each
1 lemon, halved
6 oranges, cut into ⅛-inch-thick slices (do not peel)
Kitchen twine to tie fish

Chop the fennel fronds and place in a large bowl. Using a mandoline or knife, thinly slice the fennel and add to the fronds. Stir in the olives, onion, orange slices, parsley and oil. Season well with plenty of salt and black pepper. Set aside.

Make 3 to 4 diagonal slits on the skin of each fillet. Turn over and remove any bones that remain. Season well with salt and pepper. Squeeze juice from lemon over each fillet.

Lay 4 orange slices with rinds intact in a row on a clean surface. Place one fish fillet, skin side down, on the oranges so that they run along the length of the fish. Mound half the fennel filling neatly on the fish, making sure the olives and orange slices are evenly spread out. Top with a second fillet, skin side up. Lay another 4 orange slices along the length of the fish. Using kitchen twine, tie the fish at regular 1-inch intervals, making sure the oranges are kept in place with the twine. Repeat with remaining fish, filling and oranges. (You will have extra orange slices left over for the grill.)

Place a well-oiled grill rack about 5-6 inches above the coals or heat source. Heat grill to medium-high. Place fish on rack and grill on each side for 5 minutes. Arrange about 12 orange slices on the cooler side of the grill. Place fillets on oranges, allowing them to cook more slowly. Close lid on grill and cook for an additional 30 minutes, turning once, until cooked through. (To check doneness, poke fish near an incision to see if it is white throughout.) Remove from grill. Let stand for 5 minutes. Using a sharp knife, cut each fillet into 4 large slices. Serve.

Cook's Tip: Snapper can be assembled in advance. Wrap in parchment paper, cover and refrigerate. Transport in a cooler. Let stand outside cooler for 10 minutes before grilling.

SLOW-ROASTED BABY BEETS

*The extra time these individual packets spend over the flame
gives them their deep, caramelized flavor.*

2 pounds baby golden beets
2 pounds baby red beets
1 tablespoon coriander seeds, lightly crushed
⅓ cup extra-virgin olive oil
⅓ cup Marsala wine
2 tablespoons honey
Sea salt flakes and freshly ground black pepper

Trim the leaves from the beets, then peel and cut into halves or quarters depending on size. Place in a medium bowl. Add the coriander, oil, Marsala wine and honey. Toss well to mix. Season to taste with salt and pepper.

Make 8 12-inch, double-layered squares from aluminum foil and place on a clean surface. Line each with a 10-inch square of parchment paper. Divide the beets evenly among the squares, mounding in the center. Spoon over any juices from the bowl. Fold up the sides and ends of each square to form a small rectangular pouch. Pinch ends to securely close. Be sure to leave plenty of space and air in each pouch as they will puff up as they cook.

Preheat grill to medium-hot. Place pouches on grill and cook until they begin to puff up, about 10 minutes. Shake each pouch and move to a cooler side of the grill (you may need to shift some of the coals to one side of the barbecue to make it cooler). Close grill lid and continue to cook until the beets are tender and the juices are bubbling and caramelized, about 30 minutes. Serve warm or cold.

Cook's Tip: Baby beet pouches can be assembled before cooking up to 1 day in advance.

Metal planters turned ice buckets? Seashells as salt dishes? It's enough to make you wonder why you've ever eaten anywhere but the beach.

SIMPLE (YET DIVINE!) SLICED POTATO SALAD

Simple? Indeed. Simple-tasting? Not by any stretch of the imagination.

3 pounds medium Yukon Gold potatoes
1 bunch green onions, thinly sliced
2 cups fresh flat-leaf parsley
2 cups fresh mint leaves
½ cup extra-virgin olive oil
Finely grated zest and juice of 2 lemons
Salt and freshly ground black pepper

Place a large metal pot of salted water over an open fire or stovetop. Cover and bring to a boil. Randomly pierce the potatoes with a skewer. Add to water, cover and bring back to a boil. Remove lid and continue to cook until tender, about 20-25 minutes.

Remove potatoes from water and place on a rack over an open fire. Grill until skins just begin to crisp in places, about 5-8 minutes. Remove from grill and cool slightly.

Meanwhile, place the remaining ingredients in a large bowl and toss to mix. With skins still intact, slice the warm potatoes and add to ingredients in bowl. Mix well. Let stand for 10 minutes. Season to taste with salt and pepper. Serve warm or cold.

GRILLED BLUEBERRY, PEAR + VANILLA PIZZA

Juicy blueberries, sweet pears and creamy crème fraîche.
You'll never look at pizza the same way.

2 1-pound frozen pizza doughs, thawed
2 tablespoons butter
4 tablespoons sugar
1 vanilla bean, halved lengthwise, seeds removed and set aside
2 Bosc pears, peeled, halved, cored and cut into ¼-inch-thick slices
2 pints blueberries
2 cups ricotta
2 tablespoons crème fraîche
2 tablespoons confectioners' sugar

Divide each pound of dough into 4 equal pieces. On a lightly floured surface, roll each piece into a 10-inch by 8-inch rectangle. Let stand for 2-3 minutes. If dough has shrunk, roll out again. Layer dough between sheets of floured parchment paper or plastic wrap. Set aside.

Meanwhile, make the filling. In a large skillet over a medium to medium-high grill or stovetop, melt the butter. Add the sugar, vanilla bean and seeds, stirring until sugar dissolves. Add the pears and cook until golden, about 3 minutes. Add the blueberries and cook until berries look as if they are ready to burst, about 5 minutes. Remove from heat. In a separate bowl, mix together the ricotta, crème fraîche and confectioners' sugar.

Working in batches of 2 or 3 pizzas, place each on grill and cook for 2 minutes or until bottom is golden brown. Flip pizza over and move to the cooler part of the grill. Spread a heaping ¼ cup of the ricotta mixture on pizza and top with 2-3 tablespoons of the fruit. Return to the hot part of the grill and cook for another 4 minutes or until the bottom is crisp and the filling is warmed through. Slice and serve immediately.

Cook's Tip: Pizza dough can be rolled out, covered and chilled up to 12 hours in advance.

ALL-NIGHT ALfRESCO

*Over the moon! That's how you'll feel about
these small plates served under the stars.*

PEAR + ROQUEFORT ENDIVE BOATS

Single spears of red and green endive hold scoops of creamy, crunchy goodness.

1 red Belgian endive
1 green Belgian endive
2 Bosc pears
8 ounces aged Roquefort cheese
½ cup pecans, chopped and toasted
3 tablespoons sour cream
1 tablespoon white wine vinegar
Salt and freshly ground black pepper

Trim the Belgian endive at the base and peel off each leaf; place in a bowl of ice-cold water.

Peel the pears, halve lengthwise and scoop out the seeds and core. Roughly chop the pears and place in a bowl. Crumble half the cheese over the pears. Add half the pecans to the pears. Stir in the sour cream and add the vinegar according to taste. Season with salt and pepper.

Drain the endive and pat dry with paper towels. Place 1 heaping teaspoon of filling into each leaf. Top each filled leaf with one thin slice of cheese and a small sprinkle of remaining pecans.* Serve.

*For a more unique garnish, top endive spears with shaved pecans instead. Simply chop and toast only ¼ cup of the pecans for filling mixture, then, using a mandoline or garlic shaver, shave remaining pecans and use as garnish.

Cook's Tip: *Pear filling can be made up to 4 hours in advance. Refrigerate in a bowl with plastic wrap directly over the surface to prevent discoloring. Assemble leaves up to 30 minutes before serving.*

parsley—SLICED FRUIT'S NEW BEST FRIEND

Move over lemons, there's a new brown fruit foe in town: parsley. While this leafy herb most commonly gets your kudos for adding a little oomph to sauces and stews, it can now top your list as one more thing to help keep your sliced fruit from turning brown. A few sprigs tossed in a bowl of cold water along with your cut fruit (think pears, apples, peaches and the like) will keep fresh fruit looking just that—fresh.

CRAB CAKES *with* AIOLI
+ PLANTAIN CHIPS

CRAB CAKES *with* AIOLI + PLANTAIN CHIPS

A party staple gets all dolled up with spicy aioli and crunchy plantains.

6 tablespoons unsalted butter
2 shallots, finely chopped
1 cup fresh fine breadcrumbs
2 tablespoons mayonnaise
1 tablespoon Dijon mustard
Finely grated zest and juice of 1 lemon
1 pound snow crab claw meat (3 pounds of snow crab claws give you 1 pound of meat)
½ cup tightly packed cilantro leaves, roughly chopped
½ cup tightly packed mint leaves, roughly chopped
Sea salt flakes and freshly ground black pepper
1 large egg
½ cup Panko* breadcrumbs

SMOKED AIOLI

½ cup mayonnaise
2 garlic cloves, crushed with 1 tablespoon sea salt flakes
3 tablespoons crème fraîche
1 tablespoon adobo sauce from canned chipotle peppers
2 tablespoons fresh lemon juice

PLANTAIN CHIPS

3 green plantains, peeled and sliced into ½-inch-thick slices
Vegetable oil
½ teaspoon smoked paprika
1 tablespoon sea salt flakes

Lime wedges as garnish

Preheat oven to 400°F. Heat 3 tablespoons butter in a non-stick skillet over low heat. Add the shallots and fresh breadcrumbs and sauté until shallots are just tinged with color and breadcrumbs are golden brown, about 10 minutes. Transfer to a paper towel-lined plate to drain and cool.

In a small bowl, mix together the mayonnaise, mustard, lemon zest and juice. Using a fork, gently stir in the crabmeat, followed by the herbs. Add the shallots and browned breadcrumbs. Mix well. Season to taste with salt and pepper. Gently mix in the egg.

Spray a baking sheet with non-stick cooking spray. Using hands, shape crabmeat mixture into 24 individual balls, about 1 heaping tablespoon each. Roll balls in the Panko, place on prepared baking sheet about 1 inch apart, then slightly flatten with hands. Cover loosely with plastic wrap and chill for at least 30 minutes or overnight.

Remove crab cakes from refrigerator; discard plastic wrap. Melt remaining butter and drizzle over crab cakes. Bake until crisp, golden brown and heated through, about 20 minutes.

For the Smoked Aioli: in a small bowl, mix together all the ingredients. Taste for seasoning, adding extra lemon juice and/or salt and pepper as needed. Chill until ready to serve.

For the Plantain Chips: heat the oil in a skillet (add enough to come ½ inch up sides of pan). Working in batches, add enough plantains to form a single layer in the oil. Cook until golden and just crisp, turning once, about 5 minutes. Remove from pan and drain on a paper towel-lined plate. Cool slightly. Place plantains between two sheets of parchment paper or plastic wrap and pound with a rolling pin or mallet to flatten to ¼ inch thick. Dip each plantain in ice-cold water (the water will make them extra crisp), sprinkle with smoked paprika and return to pan of hot oil. Fry for another 2 minutes on each side until golden brown. Drain on paper towels and sprinkle with salt.

To serve, place a dollop of aioli in the base of a small cup or plate, top with several plantain chips followed by 3 crab cakes. Garnish with lime wedges.

*Panko is a Japanese-style breadcrumb and is coarser and crunchier than regular breadcrumbs. Look for it in your local grocery store or Asian specialty market. If you can't find Panko, you can subsitute an equal amount of regular breadcrumbs. The only difference will be a slightly less-crunchy crab cake.

Cook's Tip: Crab cakes can be cooked up to one hour in advance. Reheat in the oven just before serving. The aioli can be made up to 24 hours in advance. Keep chilled, then return to room temperature before serving. The plantain chips can be fried and flattened several hours in advance. Fry the plantains for the second time either immediately prior to serving or up to 30 minutes before; keep warm in a low-temperature oven.

SWEET + SAVORY PETITE PANINIS

A sophisticated spin on grilled cheese that's easy to make yet impossible to resist.

1 long French baguette or sourdough ficelle
3 tablespoons unsalted butter, softened
Sea salt flakes and freshly ground black pepper
2 ounces quince jelly*
2 cups loosely packed arugula, washed, spun dry and finely chopped
8 ounces aged Manchego or Pecorino cheese, shredded

Using a bread knife, slice the bread into long, thin slices (about 8 inches long) at the longest diagonal possible, cutting 16 slices total. Butter and season with salt and pepper both sides of each slice. Set 8 slices in front of you on a clean surface.

Thinly spread the quince jelly on each of the 8 slices. Top with the arugula and then the shredded cheese. Sandwich each with a second slice of bread, pressing down with hands.

Preheat a panini sandwich maker to medium-high. Toast the sandwiches until cheese melts and bread is golden brown, about 4-5 minutes. You can also use a grill pan or skillet, pressing gently with a spatula until golden, about 2 minutes for each side. Serve whole or cut in half.

*Quince jelly can be found in most supermarkets or grocery stores. If you can't locate it, substitute either apricot or peach jelly.

Cook's Tip: *Assembled, untoasted paninis can be made up to 1 day ahead. Wrap in plastic wrap and keep refrigerated until ready to grill and serve. Toast up to 1 hour before if serving at room temperature.*

Whether your outdoor feast started out under a starry sky or one that the sun just set on, getting creative with your lighting can go a long way toward giving your scene a glowing review.

MINI LAMB CHOPS *with* MINT PEA MASH

Peas with mint and lamb with panache. Trust us, guests won't stop at just one.

8 frenched rib lamp chops (about 1½ pounds total)
Salt and freshly ground black pepper
2 tablespoons whole-grain mustard
6 tablespoons Panko breadcrumbs, crushed finer with your fingers
2 tablespoons extra-virgin olive oil

MINT PEA MASH

1 pound frozen peas
¼ cup tightly packed fresh mint leaves, finely chopped
2 tablespoons crème fraîche or sour cream

Extra mint sprigs as garnish

Preheat oven to 400°F. Set oven rack to center of oven. Season lamb with salt and pepper. Dip the meat part of each chop in the mustard, then coat with the breadcrumbs, pressing down well to secure the crumbs in place. Wrap each bone with a small piece of foil. Place on a small baking sheet and let stand at room temperature for 20 minutes.

Meanwhile, make the Mint Pea Mash. Bring a pot of salted water to a boil. Add the peas, return to a boil and cook for 5 minutes or until tender. Drain, reserving 2-4 tablespoons of the water. Place the peas in a food processor, add 2 tablespoons of the reserved cooking water. Season with salt and pepper and process until a rough puree forms (if too thick, add a little more water). Transfer mash to a bowl and fold in the mint and crème fraîche or sour cream. Season to taste with salt and pepper.

In a large oven-proof skillet, heat oil until just hot but not smoking. Add the lamb chops and cook over high heat, about 2 minutes on each side. Transfer skillet to oven and cook an additional 3 minutes or until desired doneness is reached. Remove from pan and let stand for 3 minutes.

Spoon the pea mash into one side of 8 small plates or bowls and place a lamb chop on top. Garnish with a sprig of mint and serve.

Cook's Tip: *Mint Pea Mash can be prepared up to 1 day ahead. Make the mash but do not add the mint; keep refrigerated. Heat through and stir in mint just before serving.*

MASCARPONE-STUFFED FIGS + DATES

Fresh figs and dates mingle with their most favorite things—gooey, golden honey and rich mascarpone.

4 ounces mascarpone cheese
1 tablespoon confectioners' sugar
Finely grated zest of 1 orange
2 tablespoons fresh orange juice
Pinch of fine sea salt
2 tablespoons dark or black honey
8 Medjool dates
8 ripe black or green figs
¼ cup shelled pistachios

In a small bowl, mix together the mascarpone, confectioners' sugar, orange zest and juice, salt and 1 tablespoon of the honey.

Cut a slit along the length of each date. Pull out the seed and gently ease each date slightly more open. Cut a deep "X" into each fig, being sure not to cut all the way through. Ease each fig open. Carefully spoon one teaspoon of the mascarpone filling into all of the dates and figs. Place on a serving platter or small plate.

Rub the pistachios in a paper towel to remove the skins. Finely chop the nuts. Drizzle the dates and figs with the remaining honey and sprinkle with the pistachios to serve.

Cook's Tip: The figs and dates can be cut and filled up to 4 hours ahead. Drizzle with honey and sprinkle with pistachios just before serving.

MUY BUENO MINI CARAMEL FLANS

"Very good" doesn't even begin to describe the raves you'll receive for these darling desserts.

1 cup heavy cream

2 cups whole milk

1 cinnamon stick

1 vanilla bean, halved lengthwise, seeds removed and reserved

6 tablespoons cold water

1½ cups sugar

6 large eggs

3 egg yolks

16 ¼-cup shot glasses, insides buttered

Gold leaf as garnish (optional)

In a saucepan over medium heat, combine the cream, milk, cinnamon stick, vanilla bean and seeds. Bring to a simmer. Remove from heat, cover and let stand for at least 20 minutes. Remove and discard the cinnamon stick and the vanilla bean.

In a separate saucepan, gently heat the water and 1 cup of the sugar until sugar dissolves. Bring to a boil. Continue boiling until syrup is a deep amber color, about 10 minutes. Divide equally among the prepared shot glasses. Let caramel cool completely.

Preheat oven to 350°F. Set rack to center of oven. Using an electric hand mixer fitted with a whisk attachment, whisk together the eggs, egg yolks and the remaining sugar until thick and creamy. Gradually whisk in the milk mixture. Pour into the prepared glasses, filling to the top.

Place the glasses in a deep roasting pan. Fill the pan with enough hot water to come halfway up the sides of each glass. Cover with foil. Place in oven and cook for 20 minutes or until flans are just set. Remove from oven and lift glasses out of the roasting pan. Place in refrigerator and chill overnight.

To serve, remove flans from refrigerator. Loosen sides from glasses by gently pressing down tops with finger. Turn each out, upside down, onto a small plate. (If flans don't easily release, dip glasses in a bowl of hot water for 30 seconds and carefully run a small knife along inside edge of each glass.) Chill until ready to serve, adding a piece of gold leaf on top as garnish if desired.

Cook's Tip: The flans can be made up to 2 days ahead. In fact, the longer they refrigerate in their individual glasses, the more caramel juices they will release.

BROWN BAG *it*

*Lunchtime goes lavish in this
decadent picnic for one.*

PEA, FETA + PROSCIUTTO SALAD

The crunch of prosciutto makes this cold feta and pea salad extra special.

12 ounces fresh or frozen peas
2 tablespoons light olive oil
4 wafer-thin slices prosciutto
¼ cup finely diced onion
1 garlic clove, crushed to a paste with ¼ teaspoon sea salt flakes
2 tablespoons fresh flat-leaf parsley, torn
2 tablespoons fresh oregano
¼ cup crumbled Greek feta cheese
Freshly ground black pepper

Bring a small pot of water to a boil; add the peas and cook until tender, about 3 minutes. Drain and plunge in a bowl of ice water. Let stand until cold and each pea is plump. Drain.

Meanwhile, heat the oil in a medium-sized skillet until hot. Lay the prosciutto flat in the pan and cook, turning once, over medium to high heat until crisp, about 3 minutes. Transfer to a plate and let cool. Crumble.

Add the onion to the pan juices and cook over medium to low heat until transparent, about 3 minutes. Stir in the garlic. Cook for another 5 minutes until the onion is golden in color and tender. Remove from heat and add the drained peas, crumbled prosciutto, fresh herbs and feta. Season to taste with freshly ground black pepper.

Cook's Tip: Salad can be made and refrigerated up to 1 day in advance.

OVERNIGHT CAPONATA ROLLS

Resist the temptation to sink your teeth into these as soon as they're made. A little time will make the flavors—and, thus, tomorrow's lunch—that much more tasty.

3 pints cherry or grape tomatoes

4 tablespoons water

1 garlic clove, crushed with ½ tsp sea salt flakes

1 teaspoon brown sugar

¼ cup extra-virgin olive oil

Salt and freshly ground black pepper

½ teaspoon dried red pepper flakes

1 cup finely diced eggplant

1 cup finely diced zucchini

1 cup finely diced yellow squash

2 tablespoons small raisins

1 small red onion, diced

2 tablespoons red wine vinegar

½ cup tightly packed fresh basil leaves, roughly torn

2 tablespoons chopped fresh flat-leaf parsley

3 tablespoons pine nuts, toasted

4 small square ciabatta rolls

Place the tomatoes and water in a small pot. Cover and cook on high for 15 minutes, swirling the pot to stir the tomatoes. (Tomatoes will soften and most will pop.) Remove from heat and strain through a fine-mesh sieve, pushing the tomatoes down with a rubber spatula. Discard the seeds and skin. Return the tomato mixture to the pot; add the garlic, sugar and 1 tablespoon of the oil. Bring to a boil. Reduce heat and simmer until mixture has reduced to 1 cup, about 10 minutes. Season to taste with salt and pepper. Remove from heat and set aside.

Heat the remaining oil in a skillet until just hot but not smoking. Add the pepper flakes and cook for 30 seconds. Stir in the eggplant, zucchini and squash and cook, stirring frequently, until golden brown, about 10 minutes. Add the raisins and tomato sauce and cook over medium to high heat until tender, about 10 minutes. Remove vegetable mixture from heat and set aside.

Meanwhile, mix the onion and vinegar in a small bowl. Cover and let stand for 10 minutes. Add the onion and vinegar mixture, the herbs and the toasted pine nuts to the vegetable mixture. Season caponata mixture to taste with salt and pepper. Cool completely.

Cut the rolls in half horizontally, then partially hollow out each center. Fill each half with some of the cooled caponata mixture. Top with the remaining half of each roll, pressing down slightly. Wrap in wax paper and tie with string to secure. Let stand for at least 1 hour before serving or keep chilled until ready to pack.

HOMEMADE "MARCONA" ALMONDS

A crunchy, salty snack you'll crave every day of the week.

8 ounces sliced almonds, with or without skins
2 tablespoons extra-virgin olive oil
1 tablespoon sea salt flakes

Preheat oven to 350°F. Set rack to center of oven. Spread the almonds on a large baking sheet and mix with the oil and salt. Transfer to oven and roast until almonds are golden brown, about 8-10 minutes. Toss the almonds halfway through cooking.

Remove baking sheet from oven and let cool completely. Transfer to an airtight plastic container, cover and store until ready to serve.

THE RIGHT WAY TO READ A RECIPE
(so you won't go wrong)

Believe it or not, there's a right—and, yes, a wrong—way to read a recipe. When looking through ingredient lists, pay close attention to the placement of all those "preparation modifiers" (terms such as "diced," "chopped" and "cooked"). The order in which they appear next to an ingredient is actually very important. Take, for instance, these two similar (but oh-so-different!) recipe lines:

    1 cup almonds, sliced
    1 cup sliced almonds

The first line calls for you to measure out one cup of almonds, and *then* slice them. The second calls for one cup of almonds that have *already* been sliced. Reading—and thus measuring—things correctly can be the difference between a dish that's forgettable and one that's anything but.

SAVORY ALMOND BISCUITS *with* CHEESE

Chewy, buttery cookies sandwich creamy, rich cheese for a dessert you'll want all to yourself.

1 cup Homemade "Marcona" Almonds (see page 60)
1½ cups all-purpose flour
12 tablespoons (1½ sticks) unsalted butter, at room temperature
¾ cup granulated sugar
1 large egg, beaten
½ teaspoon freshly ground black pepper
Assorted soft and hard cheeses

Coarsely chop ¼ cup Homemade "Marcona" Almonds; set aside. Put the remaining almonds in a food processor and process until ground to a fine meal. Pour into a medium bowl, sift in the flour and mix well. Set aside.

Place the butter in the bowl of a standing mixer fitted with the paddle attachment. Mix on low speed until smooth. Add the sugar, egg and pepper and beat until light but not airy. With the mixer on low, gradually add the flour mixture and beat until just combined, scraping down the sides after each addition. Turn dough onto a clean surface and roll into a ball; cover with plastic wrap and refrigerate for 30 minutes. Remove dough from refrigerator and knead gently, rolling dough into a log about 3 inches wide and 7 inches long. (For small biscuits, divide the dough in half and shape each into a log about 1½ inches wide and 7 inches long.) Spread the reserved nuts onto a baking sheet. Roll dough in almonds until thoroughly coated. Cover with plastic wrap and place in the freezer for at least 1 hour.

Preheat oven to 350°F. Set rack to center of oven. Remove the dough from the freezer and slice into ¼-inch-thick slices. If too hard, let stand at room temperature for 5 minutes. Place cut biscuits 1 inch apart on parchment-lined baking sheets. Bake for 15-18 minutes (10-12 minutes for smaller biscuits) or until edges are slightly golden in color. Do not overbake. Let biscuits stand for 5 minutes before placing on a wire rack to cool completely.

To make a cheese biscuit "sandwich," spread 1-2 tablespoons of good-quality soft cheese (such as Brie) onto one large biscuit. Top with a second biscuit, pressing down to secure. For smaller biscuits, simply serve alongside an assortment of soft and hard cheeses.

Cook's Tip: *You can always cook up smaller, more "individual-sized" batches of these biscuits. Simply slice off just as many biscuits as you'd like to bake and return remaining dough to freezer. Unsliced dough will keep in the freezer, wrapped in plastic wrap, for up to 2 weeks.*

KEYS TO SUCCESSFUL ALFRESCO DINING

or

HOW TO KEEP YOUR PICNIC FROM BEING THE PITS

DON'T LET THE HEAT SPOIL A GOOD THING. Literally. When picnicking, always mind the 2-hour rule: never leave food out for more than 2 hours. If it's over 90°F, make it 1 hour. After that, it's time to introduce all those leftovers to the bottom of the garbage bin.

THE LOWDOWN ON THE COOLDOWN. To help keep things cold until they're needed, always pack the cooler with food in the order it will be used. And never underpack a cooler. A fully packed cooler stays colder longer than a half-empty one.

MAYO OR MELONS…WHO'S THE REAL CULPRIT? When it comes to pointing the proverbial food poisoning finger, mayo typically takes the fall. And rightfully so…some of the time. Thanks to preservatives, mayo alone is actually too acidic for bacteria to grow in. It's when you mix it with all that yummy chicken and tuna that you get your bacteria field day. Melons, on the other hand, are the often-overlooked best friends of bacteria. Because they're not acidic like most fruits, bacteria like to grow and hang out on their rinds. And one slice of the knife is all it takes to turn your juicy watermelon into a real picnic spoiler. So always wash melons thoroughly before slicing, and be sure to keep the sliced pieces well chilled until ready to serve.

THE S.O.S. FOR SOGGY SANDWICHES. Keep the crunch in your crusty bread by avoiding wrapping sandwiches in plastic, which tends to trap in moisture. Instead wrap them in butcher or parchment paper.

BEE-HAVE! Keep bugs at bay with a little natural remedy—herbs. Fresh mint sprigs scattered around the edge of your picnic blanket can help keep bees away, while fresh rosemary and lemongrass can get to work on other picnic pests.

DRINKS DO DOUBLE DUTY. Let your drinks serve as both food chillers and thirst quenchers. Freeze juices, waters and teas the night before (in plastic, never glass!), then throw them in the cooler as you leave. They'll not only help chill your food, but they'll also stay cold throughout your picnic.

DINING *fine*

*Grab your candelabras and
dust off your china,
because this alfresco is all about fancy.*

SEARED SCALLOP ESCABECHE

A tangy, veggie relish and an exotic blend of spices
up the flavor factor on these savory scallops.

16 large or jumbo scallops
Fine-grain sea salt
3 tablespoons extra-virgin olive oil
4 celery stalks, julienned
1 large carrot, peeled and julienned
1 red onion, julienned
½ cup aged sherry vinegar
1 teaspoon pink peppercorns, lightly crushed

MOROCCAN SPICE MIX
3 tablespoons sesame seeds
2 teaspoons coriander seeds
1 teaspoon cumin seeds
½ cup shelled pistachios
½ tablespoon sea salt flakes

Season the scallops with salt and let stand for 10 minutes. Rub with 1 tablespoon of the oil. In a large skillet, sear the scallops for 3 minutes on each side until tops are browned and insides are just opaque. Remove and place in a large, shallow dish.

In a clean sauté pan, heat the remaining oil and add the celery, carrots and onion. Cook for 2 minutes. Add the vinegar and peppercorns and bring to a boil. Remove from heat and immediately pour over the scallops. Scallops will continue to cook and become firm. Cool completely. Cover and refrigerate overnight.

For the Moroccan Spice Mix: preheat oven to 350°F. Spread the sesame seeds on a baking sheet and toast for 7-10 minutes, or until golden brown. Remove from oven and add the coriander and cumin seeds. Toast for an additional 5 minutes. Allow spices to cool. Add to a spice grinder along with the pistachios and salt. Process until the pistachios are finely chopped and spices are well blended.

To serve, place a small mound of the julienned vegetables in the center of a plate. Top with 2 scallops and sprinkle with 1 teaspoon of the Moroccan Spice Mix.

YOU SAY ES-KEH-*behsh*. WE SAY *de-lish*.

Originally from Spain, but loved the world over (in Jamaica it's called "escovitch" and in Italy, "escabecio"), escabeche refers to a dish of poached or fried fish that's covered with an acidic marinade, left to sit for at least 24 hours, and then served cold, usually as an appetizer.

ROASTED ARTICHOKE SALAD

This all-too-pretty side salad of roasted artichokes, olives and tomatoes easily takes center stage.

8 baby or 4 medium artichokes
2 lemons
1 cup kalamata olives, halved and pitted
2 large sprigs fresh rosemary
½ cup extra-virgin olive oil
Sea salt and freshly ground black pepper
1 small red onion, finely diced
2 teaspoons sumac*
2 garlic cloves, peeled and crushed with 1 tsp sea salt flakes
3 tablespoons red wine vinegar
1 English cucumber, peeled, seeded and coarsely diced
4 ripe tomatoes, seeded and cut into large pieces
3 cups loosely packed combination of flat-leaf parsley and mint leaves

Preheat oven to 400°F. Peel 6 thin strips of lemon peel from the lemons and place in a large ceramic or glass ovenproof dish (do not use metal, as it will react with the lemon juice). Squeeze the juice from the lemons and add to the dish.

If using baby artichokes, remove the outer, tougher leaves and cut each artichoke in half. Scoop out the choke in the center and discard. If using medium-sized artichokes, remove at least half of the outer leaves and cut off the top inch of each artichoke. Quarter, scoop out the choke and discard.

Place artichoke halves in the dish with the lemon and rub with the juice to prevent from browning. Add the olives and rosemary, followed by half the oil. Mix together using your hands and season with salt and pepper. Cover the artichokes first with parchment paper, then with foil. Bake for 30 minutes. Remove covers, gently toss the artichokes and continue to cook, uncovered, for 15 minutes or until tender and just tinged with color. Remove from oven and cool slightly.

Meanwhile, in a large bowl, stir together the onion, sumac, garlic and vinegar. Let stand for 10 minutes. Stir in the cucumber and tomatoes. Add the artichokes and the contents of the roasting dish. Toss to mix, adding the remaining oil. Gently stir in the parsley and mint. Serve at room temperature.

*Sumac is a red berry that is available as a ground spice. Look for it in the spice aisle or in Turkish and Middle Eastern food shops.

Cook's Tip: *Salad can be made 1 day in advance. Prepare as above, mixing the tomatoes, cucumber, parsley and remaining oil separately. Bring to room temperature and combine with artichoke mixture (also brought to room temperature) when ready to serve.*

NUTTY ORZO HERB SALAD

Roasted nuts, savory browned butter and loads of fresh herbs make orzo out of this world.

½ cup extra-virgin olive oil
4 tablespoons unsalted butter
2 ounces vermicelli, crushed into 1-inch pieces
1 pound of orzo
4 cups hot water
2 tablespoons sea salt flakes
1 cup ice-cold water
1½ cups blanched, whole almonds
2 teaspoons freshly ground black pepper
2 cups loosely packed, finely chopped arugula
4 tablespoons finely chopped fresh tarragon
4 tablespoons finely chopped fresh flat-leaf parsley
2 tablespoons honey
Finely grated zest and juice of 2 lemons
Salt and freshly ground black pepper

In a large stock pot, heat 2 tablespoons of the oil. Add 2 tablespoons of the butter and heat until melted. Add the vermicelli. Cook over high heat until toasted, about 5 minutes. Add the orzo and cook for another 2 minutes, stirring well. Add the 4 cups of hot water and the salt and bring to a boil. Reduce heat and cook, uncovered, on medium-high for 20 minutes. Remove from heat and add the ice-cold water, mixing well. Spread pasta evenly onto 2 large baking sheets. Drizzle half of the remaining oil over pasta and gently toss to keep orzo from sticking together. Let mixture cool completely.

Meanwhile, melt the remaining butter in a large skillet over a low heat until golden brown, about 5 minutes. Add the almonds. Toss and cook until almonds are toasted and the butter is a nutty brown color, about 8 minutes. Add the pepper and cook for 1 minute more. Remove from heat and stir into orzo. Let cool completely.

Once cooled, add the arugula and herbs. In a small bowl, mix together the remaining oil, honey, lemon zest and juice. Add to the orzo and gently toss until combined. Season to taste with salt and pepper. Serve at room temperature.

Cook's Tip: *Salad can be prepared up to 1 day in advance. Store in an airtight container and chill until ready to serve. Allow to return to room temperature before serving.*

PEPPERED BEEF TENDERLOIN
with BALSAMIC-DATE GLAZE

This so-not-fussy tenderloin with glaze gets made ahead, then sliced right at the table for the perfect touch of fancy.

1 2½-pound center-cut beef tenderloin roast
2 tablespoons extra-virgin olive oil
1 tablespoon sea salt
3 tablespoons mixed peppercorns
1 tablespoon cumin seeds
1 cup full-bodied red wine
½ cup chopped Medjool dates
2 cinnamon sticks
1 vanilla bean, halved lengthwise, seeds removed and reserved
2 cups beef stock
½ cup beef or veal demi-glaze
1 tablespoon good-quality balsamic vinegar

Preheat oven to 425°F. Rub the meat with 1 tablespoon of the oil. With a mortar and pestle, lightly crush together the salt, peppercorns and cumin. Spread on a baking sheet and roll meat in the spices until evenly coated. Using butcher's string, tie the meat at 1-inch intervals. Let stand at room temperature for 20 minutes.

Heat the remaining oil in a heavy skillet over medium-high heat. Add the beef and sear for 5 minutes on each side. Transfer to a roasting pan and roast until thermometer inserted into center of tenderloin reads 120°F, about 20-25 minutes. Remove from oven and transfer to a large cutting board. Loosely cover with aluminum foil and let stand an additional 10-15 minutes, until thermometer reaches 130°F (medium-rare doneness).

Meanwhile, on a stovetop, place the roasting pan over medium-high heat. Add the wine, scraping up any loose bits. Add the dates, cinnamon, vanilla bean and seeds. Cover and cook over high heat until reduced by half. Transfer mixture to a shallow sauté pan and stir in the beef stock and demi-glaze; simmer until reduced by half, about 10-15 minutes. Add the vinegar and cook an additional 2 minutes. Remove from heat and strain into a small bowl.

To serve warm, carve the meat into ½-inch-thick slices and serve with warm sauce. To serve cold, wrap the cooled meat (unsliced) in plastic wrap, wrap again in foil and refrigerate overnight. Chill the sauce. Allow both to return to room temperature just before carving.

SUMMER BERRIES *with* ALMOND MERINGUES

Yummy clouds of almond meringue dot mounds of lush, juicy summer fruit.

SUMMER BERRIES

½ cup loosely packed dark brown sugar
1 cup water
6 kaffir lime leaves or 8 fresh sprigs of mint
2-inch piece fresh gingerroot, peeled and sliced
1 pint raspberries
1 pint blueberries
2 pints strawberries, hulled and stems removed
2 peaches or nectarines, skins intact

ALMOND MERINGUES

4 large egg whites, room temperature
4 cups confectioners' sugar, sifted
Pinch of salt
Seeds from 1 vanilla bean
2 cups sliced almonds, chopped and lightly toasted

In a small saucepan over medium heat, combine sugar and water. Heat slowly until sugar dissolves. Add 2 kaffir lime leaves (or 2 sprigs of mint) and the ginger. Bring to a boil and cook until heavy syrup forms, about 8-10 minutes. Strain and set aside, discarding solids. Meanwhile, wash and dry all the berries. (If the strawberries are small, leave whole; otherwise, halve or slice them.) Place in a large plastic bowl.

In a medium saucepan, bring several cups of water to a boil. Add the peaches or nectarines and boil for 1 minute. Drain and rinse under cold water. Peel and discard the skins. Cut the fruit into wedges and add to the berries.

If using kaffir lime leaves, remove the middle vein from the remaining leaves and discard. Slice into thin shreds and add to the berries. (If using mint, slice just the leaves and discard the stems.) Pour the warm syrup over the berries and toss to coat. Let stand for at least 1 hour. Once cooled, cover and chill until ready to serve.

Meanwhile, make the meringues. Preheat oven to 350°F. Line 2 baking sheets with parchment paper. Place egg whites in a medium, heatproof bowl set over a pot of simmering water (do not allow the bowl to touch the water). Stir in the sugar and salt. Using an electric hand mixer, whisk the mixture until an instant thermometer reads 120°F, about 5 minutes. Remove the bowl from the pot and continue to whisk until the mixture is thick and glossy and very stiff peaks form. Gently fold in the vanilla seeds and toasted almonds.

Spoon heaping teaspoonfuls of the meringue mixture onto the prepared baking sheet, about 1 inch apart. Place in oven, keeping door slightly ajar. Bake until meringues slightly puff up and crack around the sides, about 15-20 minutes. Meringue should feel dry on the outside and slightly soft inside. Remove from oven and cool completely on a wire rack. Serve with berries.

Cook's Tip: Berries can be prepared up to 1 day in advance. Covered and stored in an airtight container, meringues can be made up to 2 weeks in advance.

FOR THE GRILL *of* IT

Fire up the grill, ladies.
An entire menu of skewered eats makes
this backyard BBQ one for the gals.

STUCK ON ANTIPASTO

These one-bite wonders lend a touch of the unexpected to traditional antipasto.

4 ounces provolone cheese, unsliced
4 ounces thinly sliced salami, rind removed
4 ounces pitted or stuffed green olives
4 ounces feta cheese
16 large fresh basil leaves
16 cherry tomatoes—red, yellow or orange
⅓ cup extra-virgin olive oil
2-3 tablespoons good-quality balsamic vinegar
Freshly ground black pepper
32 long bamboo skewers

For the salami, provolone and olive skewers: cut provolone into ¼-inch-thick sticks, each about 1½ inches long. Wrap each stick of provolone with one slice of salami. Assemble skewers by threading one olive followed by one piece of salami-wrapped provolone onto each skewer. Repeat, making 16 skewers.

For the feta, basil and tomato skewers: cut feta into chunks, each about ½ inch by 1 inch. Wrap each piece of feta with one basil leaf. Assemble skewers by threading one piece of basil-wrapped feta followed by one cherry tomato onto each skewer. Repeat, making 16 skewers.

In a small, shallow bowl, whisk together the olive oil and balsamic vinegar. Season to taste with freshly ground black pepper. Serve as a dip alongside antipasto skewers.

Cook's Tip: *The Mint Pesto from page 82 makes a great second dip for these skewers.*

SKEWERED SHRIMP *with* MINT PESTO

Jumbo prawns get seared in their shells, then dipped in a refreshing mint pesto.

24 whole, raw jumbo shrimp, deveined with shells intact
½ teaspoon dried red pepper flakes
Finely grated zest and juice of 4 limes or 2 lemons
3 tablespoons extra-virgin olive oil

MINT PESTO DIP
4 tablespoons pine nuts, toasted
4 tablespoons finely grated Pecorino cheese
½ teaspoon dried red pepper flakes
1 cup firmly packed fresh mint leaves
1 cup firmly packed fresh, flat-leaf parsley
Finely grated zest and juice of ½ a lemon
¼ cup extra-virgin olive oil
Salt and freshly ground black pepper

24 bamboo skewers, soaked in water for 20 minutes

For the shrimp: place shrimp in large, non-metallic bowl. Stir in the pepper flakes, lime or lemon zest and juice, and oil. Mix together using your hands, making sure the mixture gets under the shells of the shrimp. Cover tightly and refrigerate for at least 30 minutes and up to 4 hours.

Meanwhile, make the Mint Pesto Dip. Combine pine nuts, Pecorino, pepper flakes and herbs in a food processor. Process until finely chopped. Add the lemon zest and juice, processing again for 30 seconds. With the processor still running, slowly add the oil until well combined. Season to taste with salt and pepper. Transfer dip to a small bowl.

Thread each shrimp onto a skewer. Preheat grill to medium (you should be able to hold your hand over the heat for about 5-6 seconds). Brush grill rack liberally with oil. Place shrimp on the grill, cooking 3-4 minutes on each side. Sprinkle lightly with salt and pepper while cooking. Do not overcook. Shrimp will pinken and edges will be slightly crisp when done. The shrimp can be peeled while still on the skewer, then dipped into the pesto.

Cook's Tip: Refrigerated in an airtight container, *Mint Pesto Dip* can be made up to *1 day in advance.*

CHICKEN CAESAR SALAD SKEWERS

Salad on a skewer? You might never want to eat your caesar any other way.

1 pound boneless, skinless chicken breasts
4 tablespoons extra-virgin olive oil
Finely grated zest and juice of 1 lemon
2 tablespoons freshly grated Parmesan cheese
Salt and freshly ground black pepper
8 slices smoked bacon
8 ounces sourdough bread
1 teaspoon finely chopped fresh rosemary

DRESSING
4 salted anchovy fillets in oil
2 garlic cloves, peeled and crushed with 1 teaspoon sea salt flakes
3 tablespoons finely grated Parmesan cheese
1 tablespoon white wine vinegar
4 tablespoons sour cream
5 tablespoons extra-virgin olive oil
Freshly ground black pepper
1 head romaine lettuce

16 bamboo skewers, soaked in water for 20 minutes
Parmesan cheese shavings as garnish

Place each breast between 2 sheets of plastic wrap and pound with a rolling pin until flattened to about ¼ inch thick. Slice chicken breasts into strips, each about 1 inch wide and 4-5 inches long.

In a shallow glass bowl, mix together 2 tablespoons of the oil and half of the lemon zest and juice. Add the Parmesan. Season to taste with salt and pepper. Add chicken. Cover with plastic wrap and marinate at room temperature for 20 minutes or refrigerate for up to 3 hours. Bring to room temperature 10-15 minutes before using.

Meanwhile, stretch the bacon. Place each piece of bacon flat on a chopping board. Using the back of a knife, gently scrape along each strip several times until doubled in length. Set aside. Cut the bread into 1-inch cubes. Mix together the rosemary and the remaining olive oil, lemon zest and juice. Drizzle over bread cubes.

For the dressing: remove anchovies from oil. With a mortar and pestle, thoroughly mash the anchovies; add the garlic and continue to mash. Add the Parmesan, mashing until mixture is creamy. Transfer to small bowl and mix in the vinegar, followed by the sour cream. Gradually add the oil. Season to taste with pepper. Using the middle to inner leaves, trim the romaine and place leaves in a bowl of cold water. Drain immediately before serving.

Preheat grill to medium-high. Brush rack with oil and set about 4-5 inches away from the coals or heat. Assemble skewers: place a piece of bacon flat on a work surface and line with a strip of chicken. Pierce the strip with one end of the skewer, add a piece of bread, then wrap the chicken and bacon halfway around the bread. Continue wrapping the strip around the bread cubes until finished skewer is a zigzag of chicken and bacon around 3 bread pieces. Repeat with remaining bacon, chicken and bread, making 16 skewers.

Place skewers on grill and cook until chicken is tender and bread is toasted, about 3 minutes for each side. Serve each skewer in a lettuce leaf drizzled with dressing. Garnish with Parmesan shavings.

A GAL'S GUIDE TO GRILLING

GET GLOWING

Heating up that grill—not to mention your icy relationship with those coals—is as easy as ready, set, glow.

1. Begin by stacking the coals in a small pile, two or three deep, in the center of the grill.

2. Light with a match in several places (you can also use newspaper or kindling, but never use lighter fluid).

3. Let the coals burn until they have a slight red glow and more than two-thirds are ashed over (this should take about 20-30 minutes).

4. Spread the coals in a single layer, leaving an area of the grill free of coals so you can have hotter and cooler temperatures to grill over.

GRILLING, DONE WELL

So how do you know rare from medium and well-done from way overdone? Actually, it's all in the hand.

FOR RARE: Dangle one hand freely, relaxing it completely. With the forefinger of your other hand, touch the meaty area between your thumb and forefinger. This is what a rare piece of meat should feel like.

FOR MEDIUM: Make a fist with your hand. Touch the same place again. This is what a medium piece of meat should feel like.

FOR WELL-DONE: Tightly clench your fist. Touch the same place again. This is what a well-done piece of meat should feel like.

MAKE YOUR (GRILL) MARK

Use these simple tips and tricks, and you'll be one step closer to grilling guru-ness.

ALWAYS START WITH A CLEAN GRILL. Brushing your grill clean while it's still hot allows all the crusts to scrape off easily and burn into the coals.

NO BRUSH? NO PROBLEM. Can't find (or just don't have) a good heat-resistant brush for oiling up your grill? Use a raw potato half instead. Using long metal tongs, simply dip the flat side of one potato half in olive oil, then use it as a "brush" to rub over the grill rack.

UP THE FLAVOR QUOTIENT. Use dried or fresh herbs to impart added flavor to your food. Simply soak and drain the herbs (we like bay leaves, thyme, sage and rosemary), then sprinkle them over the hot coals right before grilling.

SURF + TURF ON A STICK

It's surf and turf for the girls in this duo of shrimp and beef wrapped in crispy lettuce.

1 pound sirloin or rump steak, at least 1-2 inches thick
24 large shrimp, peeled, deveined and halved horizontally

MARINADE
2 tablespoons sesame oil
Finely grated zest and juice of 1 lime
3 tablespoons soy sauce
1 tablespoon honey

VEGGIE SLAW
1 large carrot, peeled and julienned
8 ounces white radish, peeled and julienned
1 English cucumber, peeled, seeded and julienned
1 small red onion, halved and thinly sliced
2 tablespoons salt
½ cup rice wine vinegar
2 tablespoons sugar
1 green Thai chili or serrano pepper, finely chopped
1 head iceberg or Bibb lettuce, leaves separated
1 cup raw peanuts, toasted, skinned and chopped

24 bamboo skewers, soaked in water for 20 minutes

Put meat in freezer for 20 minutes. Remove and slice against the grain into long, thin strips, each about 1 inch wide and 3-4 inches long. Place meat between 2 sheets of plastic wrap or parchment paper and pound with a rolling pin to flatten. Put meat in medium bowl and set aside.

Place shrimp halves between 2 sheets of plastic wrap or parchment paper and gently pound with a rolling pin to flatten. Put shrimp in medium bowl and set aside.

In a small bowl, whisk together the sesame oil, lime zest and juice, soy sauce and honey. Divide marinade equally between steak and shrimp, mixing well. Cover with plastic wrap and marinate at room temperature for 20 minutes or refrigerate for up to 3 hours. Return to room temperature before using.

For Veggie Slaw: place first four ingredients in colander and sprinkle with salt. Let stand for 20 minutes. Meanwhile, heat the vinegar, sugar and chili in a small saucepan over medium heat until sugar dissolves. Bring to a boil. Remove from heat and set aside. Rinse vegetables in colander to remove salt. Pat dry with paper towels. Place vegetables in small bowl and toss with vinegar mixture. Cover and chill for at least 1 hour or overnight. Drain before serving.

Preheat grill to medium-high. Brush rack with oil and set about 4-5 inches away from the coals or heat. Assemble skewers: lay a piece of steak flat on a clean surface; top with flattened shrimp and thread onto a skewer as if stitching together. Repeat to make 24. Place skewers on grill and cook until meat reaches desired doneness and shrimp pinkens, about 2-3 minutes on each side.

Fill lettuce cups with one spoonful of Veggie Slaw, top with a skewer of beef and shrimp, then sprinkle with chopped peanuts. Have guests pull out skewer and wrap lettuce around filling just before eating.

CHOCOLATE-CHERRY KABOBS
with HAZELNUT COOKIES

CHOCOLATE-CHERRY KABOBS
with HAZELNUT COOKIES

Expect to lose your mind over this chocolate-stuffed cherry, cream and cookie concoction.

HAZELNUT COOKIES

1½ cups all-purpose flour
½ cup good-quality cocoa powder
Pinch of salt
1½ sticks unsalted butter, room temperature
¾ cup granulated sugar
1 egg yolk, beaten
1 teaspoon vanilla extract
½ cup hazelnuts, chopped

CHERRIES

2 pounds fresh, ripe large cherries, pitted, stems removed
4 tablespoons chocolate-hazelnut spread
2 tablespoons honey
1 cinnamon stick
½ cup water

CREAM

1 cup heavy cream
2 tablespoons confectioners' sugar, sifted
½ cup crème fraîche

24 bamboo skewers

Sift the flour, cocoa powder and salt together in a medium bowl. Using an electric mixer fitted with the paddle attachment, beat butter on low until smooth. Add the sugar, egg and vanilla and beat until light. With mixer on low, gradually add the flour mixture until just combined, scraping down sides with each addition. Divide the dough in half; roll each half into a small ball, cover with plastic wrap and refrigerate for 30 minutes. Remove dough and knead gently, rolling each half into a log about 1½ inches thick and 7 inches long. Spread the hazelnuts onto a baking sheet and gently roll each log in the hazelnuts to coat. Cover with plastic wrap and freeze for at least 1 hour.

Preheat oven to 350°F. Set rack to center of oven. Remove the cookie logs from the freezer and slice into ¼-inch-thick slices. If the dough is too hard to slice, let stand at room temperature for 5 minutes. Place cut cookies 1 inch apart on parchment-lined baking sheet and bake for 12 minutes. Do not overbake. Base of cookies should be slightly tinged with color and the nuts toasted. Let cookies stand for 5 minutes before placing on a wire rack to cool completely.

Meanwhile, prepare the cherries. Spoon the chocolate-hazelnut spread into a piping bag fitted with a ⅛-inch-diameter tip. Pipe the spread into each cherry until full. Refrigerate until needed (can be made up to 1 day in advance).

Place cream in a small bowl and sift in the confectioners' sugar. Add the crème fraîche and whisk until soft peaks form. Spoon into a serving bowl and chill until needed.

Heat the honey, cinnamon and ½ cup water in a small saucepan over medium heat for 5 minutes or until liquid forms a light syrup. Remove from heat and transfer to a small bowl. Thread 3 cherries on each skewer. Place the cherries on a medium-high grill and grill for 2 minutes on each side, brushing with the honey syrup. As soon as the cherries sizzle and the chocolate filling starts to melt, remove from grill. To serve, place 1 cookie on a small plate, top with a dollop of cream and a cherry skewer.

Cook's Tip: You can always cook up smaller batches of this dessert. Simply slice off just as many cookies as you'd like to bake and return remaining dough to freezer. Unsliced dough will keep in the freezer, wrapped in plastic wrap, for up to 2 weeks.

PICNIC-PERFECT GINGER PLUM FIZZ

This refreshingly fizzy summer spritzer—and all the yummy variations it can take—is the exclamation point for your picnic.

1 cup honey

1 3-inch piece fresh ginger, peeled and chopped

1 lemon

2½ cups water

4 red plums, halved, pitted and processed into a puree

Seltzer or sparkling water

Combine the honey and ginger in a medium saucepan. Using a vegetable peeler, remove 3 thin strips of lemon peel from the lemon. Add to the saucepan along with the juice from the lemon. Stir in the water and gently heat until simmering. Simmer for 10 minutes. Remove from heat, cover and let cool, allowing flavors to infuse.

Once cool, strain mixture through a fine-mesh sieve. Discard the ginger and lemon peel. (You will have approximately 3 cups syrup.) Stir in the plum puree. Chill. To serve, fill 8 tall glasses with ice. Add ¼ cup plum mixture to each and top with ½ cup seltzer or sparkling water.

Cook's Tip: In the mood for a refreshing lemonade instead? Thinking something with strawberries might suit your mood better? Creating variations on this picnic thirst-quencher is easy. Simply puree or squeeze the juice from your favorite fruit (some of our faves include lemons, limes, watermelon, peaches, nectarines, strawberries, raspberries, apricots and plums) and strain it through a fine-mesh sieve to make it extra smooth. Add a combination of light syrup (we've included a basic recipe below) and ½ cup sparkling water or seltzer to ¼ cup of the fruit puree and you've got the perfect picnic drink.

Light Syrup: Place 1 cup of sugar or honey in a saucepan along with 2½ cups water and a sprig of your favorite herb (we've listed some great combinations below). Add 3 strips of fresh lemon peel and the juice from 1 lemon (you can also substitute oranges or limes). Heat gently until sugar dissolves. Bring to a boil, reduce heat and simmer for 10 minutes. Remove from heat, cover and let stand for 30 minutes. Strain solids and let cool. Chill. Makes 3 cups.

Herb + Fruit Combos: Mint and lemon verbena go great with watermelon, strawberries and raspberries. Rosemary and thyme are excellent with nectarines, lemons, peaches and apricots. Ginger matches perfectly with plums or watermelon.

NOTES

NOTES

Notes

NOTES

NOTES